LIAM DAVIES

The Art of Manipulation

Your Easy Guide To Understand The Art Of Manipulation And Persuasion, Covert Emotional Manipulation Methods, And Body Language Signals

Copyright © 2021 Liam Davies

All rights reserved.

© **Copyright 2021 - All rights reserved.**

The content contained within this book may not be reproduced, duplicated or transmitted without direct written permission from the author or the publisher.

Under no circumstances will any blame or legal responsibility be held against the publisher, or author, for any damages, reparation, or monetary loss due to the information contained within this book. Either directly or indirectly.

Legal Notice:

This book is copyright protected. This book is only for personal use. You cannot amend, distribute, sell, use, quote or paraphrase any part, or the content within this book, without the consent of the author or publisher.

Disclaimer Notice:

Please note the information contained within this document is for educational and entertainment purposes only. All effort has been executed to present accurate, up to date, and reliable, complete information. No warranties of any kind are declared or implied. Readers acknowledge that the author is not engaging in the rendering of legal, financial, medical or professional advice. The content within this book has been derived from various sources. Please consult a licensed professional before attempting any techniques outlined in this book.

By reading this document, the reader agrees that under no circumstances is the author responsible for any losses, direct or indirect, which are incurred as a result of the use of information contained within this document, including, but not limited to, — errors, omissions, or inaccuracies.

Table of Content

Introduction 5

Chapter 1. Psychological Manipulation 11

Chapter 2. Turning the Tables 17

Chapter 3. Stages of a Relationship with a Covert Narcissist........ 23

Chapter 4. Covert Emotional Manipulation Methods 29

Chapter 5. Knowing Yourself 35

Chapter 6. Psychological Tricks to Examine Human Beings 41

Chapter 7. Basic Body Language Signals 47

Chapter 8. Strengthen or Change the Views of Others 53

Chapter 9. The Art of Persuasion 59

Chapter 10. Influence Without Manipulation 66

Chapter 11. Escape or Die 73

Conclusion... 79

Introduction

Once you have gotten a decent read on a person, the step to mastering your environment and analyzing your potential in each situation is learning how to manipulate another person's feelings and reactions through subtler cues, both verbal and non-verbal. This will create an environment where your suggestions can thrive.

Don't beat yourself up for thinking outside the box when it comes to analyzing and influencing people. While some people might call it manipulation, you can simply tell them that you are extremely persuasive. What's more, there is nothing to say that the person you are influencing wasn't waiting for an excuse to move forward in the direction you suggested anyway. It is your creativity in constructing a good plan or formula that turns resistance into compliance.

Besides emotion, successful manipulation is all about the imbalance of power. There may be times when getting what you want from another person means using the home-court advantage, which means keeping the person in an environment where you have primary control. This includes your home, car, office, or even your side of town. This makes it harder for your target to do things such as dodge a conversation or even decide that they think they might hurt your feelings.

While it may seem surprising, letting people dominate the conversation is a good thing when you want to have the upper hand with them. You can establish their underlying weaknesses and strengths by listening to their stories and throwing in limited questions from time to time, which will also ingratiate you to them further. It makes you look as though you are supremely interested in what they have to say. However, you don't want the conversation to be one-sided, which means you want to tell them enough about your situation to make them feel comfortable, while at the same time hiding any information that weakens your point of view or that can be contorted to mean something else. Don't be afraid to lie to protect any weaknesses in your argument.

If someone is pushing you for more than they need, you can use a humble tone and explain that there are things about your no one would understand or that you aren't interesting enough to warrant talking about. This will make them curious, and it will also make them a little nurturing, which is where you can snag them. This is known as flipping the script, and it can be a very effective technique when used selectively.

Suppose you have to speak about facts and statistics. Ramble about as many as you can to be a bit overwhelming. At this time, you need to show interest in their part but establish that if you are to go along with whatever they are suggesting, you will have your own rules. Depending on the state you are currently in, this may be enough for them to "decide" to complete the task in question or give in to your suggestion because it is easier than going along with your stipulations.

Another way to manipulate a person is to change the modulation of your voice. If you are trying to intimidate a person, you will want to be loud. If you are seeking sympathy, lose the loud tone for a depressed, defeated tone instead. Most people are inclined to help a person who is feeling down. Now that you have their sympathy, ask for something. Suggest what you want in a way that seems impossible to achieve. Wait for their response, which should be some variation of, "I want to help you." Some people will want to offer up advice as a way to soothe you. To avoid losing control of the situation, you will need to consider their advice and find that their logic is faulty to ensure things remain under your control.

Manipulation Tools for Specific Situations

A key to pulling off any form of manipulation is to see what drives the person you are dealing with. For example, is it a religion? If so, you would need to focus on their devotion and find a creative way to get your point across using their religion. It is a good way to reinforce their opinion of themselves, most likely that they are godly and intelligent. As long as you focus on their utopian visions and aspirations, you will find this technique to be very effective.

Another tool that is useful from time to time is sarcasm. It allows you to express your discontent with someone while maintaining a doorway out as if you were just joking. However, be cautious, as sarcasm can be insulting and hurtful if misused. After you have been given a chance to vent, turn it around to the sarcastic "what if." This allows the person to hear your opinion, and it comes across like you are just defeated. Now they can save you. When they offer their help, humbly tell them it is not their responsibility, but that you need their support. It is helpful to add, "What would I do without you?"

You must keep in mind that you are being manipulated every day. The news, media, and those in power all deploy tactics to keep your attention or threaten your security for non-compliance. You are bombarded with images and stories that tug at your heart, anger your soul, and move you either into action or into seclusion. Just seeing how easily you can have the same effect on a person will allow you to recognize when it is being done to you. Awareness is life-changing. At this moment, you realize you have tried conventional methods of persuasion, being genuine and truly caring. Formerly, you got nothing in return, but you will from now on.

Be Creative

You will need to focus on your creativity for these manipulative tactics. Your goal is to transform someone's reality and alter their beliefs. Every situation is different, which means you will need to be creative and think on your feet. You must observe the cues a person is giving you. You must observe their reactions to you and others, as these can be very telling. Sometimes, just watching your target interact with others can give you more insight into how to manipulate them.

For example, if you see how a coworker reacted to a customer, you can use that to make them feel justified by adding your opinion to explain how they reacted. They will repeat the excuse you provided them. This can be used against them. If you are trying to get them to do something for you, just point out how they overreacted to that customer, which should shame them into following your suggestion. They should act in the way you suggest to minimize their past actions.

Sometimes all you have to do is create an image. Think of a spin on something that would suggest the person you are dealing with is a victim. Encourage them to see how others have been unappreciative and lazy compared to them. Suggest a course of action and reap the benefits.

If you are dying to know what someone feels about a situation, for example, in politics or religion, make up a story that you read on the internet that is sure to rile them up. Sit back, watch their reaction, and start agreeing with them. Be sure to add your perspective to draw them out of the shocking story into your plan. You might just be harvesting information to keep a profile on someone who is a threat to your vision of success. Building your profile, you will be able to understand their weakness in most situations.

Take Your Time

You can be sure to pay special attention to their strengths and find ways to undermine them. Don't proceed it so far as to where others observing can figure out what your intentions are, and instead always take the high road in public so that at the end of the day, most people will only ever see the public face you decide to show them.

Keep in mind that everyone just wants to be happy, which means they seek to understand and support people around them. They think it is rare for someone to take an interest in them without wanting something in return. This is where patience becomes your ally. You cannot act like someone has to be available at a moment's notice. Anyone can figure out that you have selfish motives if you display this impatient tendency. It might be killing you to lie in wait for the perfect opportunity, but it would kill you more to be seen as a fake. So, wait. Even encourage them to ask others about the situation. Once you have proven that you are only worried about them or want to see them succeed, then you can wiggle into their mind with subtle manipulation.

While playing on the heartstrings of another, you weaken their response. You cannot simply ignore that they might say no to your request or idea. You have to come across as genuine in trying to help or care about them. Find a way to make their "no" seem unreasonable without saying it directly. You will have to point out that if someone else acted as they did, they would see it as being stubborn or pig-headed with their closed mind. Let them know that the brain has a chemical response to doing something new and brave. Tell them that the brain lights up like a Christmas tree when changes are occurring.

The bottom line is that there is potential for manipulation. It is a creative process. It takes a little planning and observing, but if mastered, it can change your life. You will feel powerful every day. You will start to see every rejection as a canvas. It is your starting point. A word for word or gesture-by-gesture guarantee that you are in control.

Self-preservation is an important aspect of manipulation. You do not want to be perceived as a manipulator. You want to be known as the neutral person who sees all sides but uses logic to decide why your decision is more valid. Maintain a solid reputation for being thoughtful, and people will seek your opinion often. This is an advantage from the start. In a new group of people, you can find a way to agree with everyone and make a statement that you were always taught to show respect and think of all sides before making a decision.

Chapter 1. Psychological Manipulation

Covert psychological manipulation is essential to the art of dark psychology. Many of the methods utilized with dark psychology will utilize this type of emotional manipulation, whether in part or entirely. As you learn a bit more about the world of dark psychology and its various symptoms, you will soon begin to see the signs of CPM. This is why it is so crucial to comprehend what CPM is precisely so that you can watch out for it in your daily life.

Covert psychological manipulation, or CPM, will attempt by a single person to attempt and influence the feelings and ideas of the other person in a manner that is considered deceptive and undiscovered by the one who is being manipulated. Being able to break down each of the words in CPM is very important to help you understand this subject's structures. Covert refers to the way that a manipulator can conceal their intentions. They wish to have the ability to hide the true nature of all their actions. Remember that not all types of influence and psychological manipulation will be classified as hidden. The victims of the concealed type, though, will usually not realize they are being controlled and will not have the ability to comprehend the way the manipulation is performed. Sometimes, they are not even able to look and determine the motivation of their manipulator.

This is why CPM is such a stealth bomber in the world of dark psychology. Its point is to prevent detection and defense up until it is far too late for the victim. The psychological side of the manipulator is going to be the specific focus of that manipulator. Other kinds of manipulation might include things like the other person's self-discipline, beliefs, and habits. Numerous manipulators will concentrate on this area of impact as they know that the other person's feelings are essential to the other elements of their character. Being able to manipulate the feelings of the other individual is essential. If a person has emotional control over the other individual, they will have complete control over them. The last piece of CPM is manipulation. It is typically thought that manipulation and impact are the same things. This is not true, though. Manipulation refers to the surprise and underhand process of influence outside the awareness of the one who is being controlled.

The objective behind this compared to someone who has the intent to influence can be a huge difference. They will enter into this with an influencer with the idea of "I wish to assist you in deciding that benefits you." With the manipulator, they have the thoughts of "I want to control you to supply advantage to myself secretly." As you can see, both of these are quite a bit different, so comprehending the objective behind any offered behavior is going to be a big part of choosing whether the scenario is hidden psychological manipulation or not.

Manipulative Circumstances

There are four primary situations in which CPM can take place. These consist of the household, romantic, individual, and professional parts of your life. Among the most typical kinds of CPM is romantic, and it can sometimes be the deadliest. There are some less obvious kinds of CPM that you can discover anywhere, and because they are less typical, they can often be the most unsafe. A good example of CPM is a managing romantic partner. If a woman remains in a relationship and her partner is trying to control her, she will be revolted by what is going on as soon as she figures it out. She might wish to discover a way to leave the circumstance. Thus, many times the controlling partner is going to exercise their impact as covertly as possible. They don't desire their partner to understand they are being managed, or the victim leaves, and there is nobody delegated control. If the manipulator achieves success, their spouse or sweetheart will continue to be a psychological manipulation victim. They might have difficulty recognizing that it is going on. This permits the manipulator to keep the control that they want with no danger of being found and losing the other person for good.

This can likewise occur with a buddy who would use CPM to get the outcomes they want when they have a relationship with another individual. In this group, one of the common types of manipulators will be covertly induced feelings of obligation, compassion, and guilt in a pal. The friend is being controlled in this way without understanding that they are being influenced. They may understand that they are acting differently to that buddy; however, they won't have the ability to explain why and how. You will discover that the expert part of your life can be another place for hidden emotional manipulators. Many people have worked for an employer or another person who had authority, who seems to set off some unidentified sensations of duty, worry, and regret in them.

Individuals who are manipulated in this manner might never identify why these feelings exist or where they come from, and in the world of CPM, the family can be the most troublesome. A proficient manipulator can discover a victim, even within their household, and the amount of influence they exercise can be dangerous. This is because the manipulator and the victim will have a very deep connection together. After all, they are related. When blood relations are included, the amount of influence and control can increase a fair bit. These family circumstances are so matched to utilizing CPM because most people currently feel a social responsibility to help their own family. They are willing to go a little more to guarantee the requirements of their family are addressed. Because of this predisposition, covert psychological manipulative practices will give you a malleable victim.

The (Bad) Love Giver

This consists of the severe, unforeseen, and robust expression of positive feelings towards a victim. It may, in the beginning, seem counterintuitive. Why do they behave so intensively positive at first if that individual is attempting to damage them? Since it matches its functions—that's why! This produces a deep sense of self-confidence, affection, and appreciation from a specific victim to their manipulator, and this is the principle behind love providing. Based on the manipulator's analysis, the degree to which enjoy providing is utilized, and the people on whom it is pre-owned forms the basis. A lonely, helpless victim who seeks help and consolation is most likely to be more love-bombed by the manipulator because the manipulator will know the victim will be more responsive to it. The more the victim is grounded, the less effort the manipulator will have to put into positivity. The meaning of the love giving technique offers two essential lessons on Emotional Manipulation. Firstly, the covert nature of Emotional Manipulation is well shown. Envision is trying to comprehend that love giving is an unfortunate thing. "Well, this guy was very sweet to me, and he made me feel very good." The red flags or warning signs of abuse are unlikely to be raised by such a declaration. This is a textbook example of how something can be provided as something favorable but has a negative result. The second general lesson pertinent to Emotional Manipulation that can be learned from love offering is how emotional manipulation is formed to suit every unique circumstance. Experienced manipulators have discreetly tested and learned from lots of encounters in their history. In any given scenario, you understand the strength and timing of each Emotional Manipulation strategy.

What is Empathy

Empathy is the capability to put yourself in another person's shoes and consider their emotions and sensations. An empath is an individual who can interact with others on several levels to experience their emotional wellness with precision. How empaths have this capacity has yet to be comprehended to many individuals, but numerous believe it is innate and transmitted through our DNA. As for how it runs, everything in deep space resonates with electrical energy; empaths are believed to can perceiving the shifts in the electrical energy around them. Empaths are usually considered compassionate, loving, sensitive to other individuals' feelings, and sympathetic. Would you be astonished to learn there's a dark side to being an empath? The essence of compassion itself makes sure that lots of are helped and supported by an empath. It likewise means empaths can see the world a lot more than we do, and as such, issues can happen in various areas of their lives. The dark side of empaths is that their sensations can't be managed. You might believe they are well versed in emotions, but the truth is they are in a constant fight to keep them under control. Sometimes, it can bring them down to depression since they so strongly feel others' feelings, specifically others' grief. They discover it difficult to separate their feelings and others and find other empaths to reveal their sensations. Empaths can accommodate a large amount of information from their sensitivity to electrical energy when managing negative energy resulting in fatigue. This can puzzle and exhaust them badly while attempting to understand everything. They are particularly prone to negative energy, as it greatly upsets them. They will easily end up being tired when all they can feel is negative energy. They are used by the less scrupulous amongst us because empaths are compassionate individuals who always believe in people's good nature. Empaths are generous and kind; they will attract only those who take and never return.

An empath can quickly fall under deep anxiety when they discover they have been conned. Because empathy tends to give to others instead of getting, it is most likely that they overlook their wellness, including their bodies and minds. This is the dark side all frequently since it's all too easy to forget how to appreciate them because of the pressure of what they feel. They keep back a little piece of their heart just if they're wounded in the future.

They can't permit themselves to fall deeply in love because they are terrified of all that love. After all, it could be a lot for them to manage.

Empaths are selfless people who are day-to-day bombarded with sensory info, so they typically feel like they carry a heavy load.

Chapter 2. Turning the Tables

Whether you're the victim or the one who is doing the manipulating, there's one thing that's for certain. Manipulation is abusive, and no one, especially not the victim, deserves to be subjected to that kind of treatment. Since most manipulators are unlikely to see the error of their ways or want to become a better person, it is up to the victim to do what they can to keep themselves as safe as possible. Cutting all ties with the manipulator will not always be immediate or easy; some relationships take time before you can sever the bonds and walk away for good. In the meantime, what do you need to do to protect yourself from being taken advantage of in that way? Perhaps turn the tables and deflect the manipulator's techniques can onto them.

Manipulation is an emotional and mental game of cat and mouse, but just because you may be the mouse in the scenario, it doesn't mean you're completely at their mercy. The savvy mouse with a few useful strategies up their sleeve can flip things around and take the power dynamic away from the manipulator. Just when the manipulator thinks they have you within their grasp, turn the tables on them and let them know you're not going to tolerate whatever it is they're trying to do to you. It's time to gain payback on the manipulator and let them know you're not as easily fooled as they might think.

Shut down the manipulator's attempts by standing up for your fundamental rights. Among the fundamental human rights that we are all entitled to include the right to be respected, the right to say no without having to feel guilty about it, the right to express your opinions and your feelings, and the right to protect yourself when you feel you might be threatened emotionally, physically or mentally among other things. These basic rights are what you need to remember when fighting back against manipulation because we so often tend to forget when we let others pressure us and play on our emotions to get their way. We forget that we have a right to protect our hearts, minds, and bodies from the people who would trample all over us if given a chance. Make these rights part of the boundaries that you set in your dealings with others, and strengthen your defenses against the manipulator using the following techniques:

Say No, Thank You - Do not feel guilty if you have to say no to the manipulator. They're trying to take advantage of you, and you are well within your rights to say no to them. They do not have any rights to pressure you into deciding or taking action with something you're not comfortable with, and when you firmly say no, remember that you don't owe them an explanation. You can make your own decisions, your own choices, and if you choose to say no, go right ahead. Some manipulators will still attempt to push the boundaries and try to persist despite you telling them no, and you're going to have to be firm and stand your ground. Make it politely but firmly clear that you're not going to change your mind, and you would appreciate it if they could respect your decision. Say no, thank you, and end the conversation there and then.

Saying No to Buy Time - If you have ever been pressured into deciding on the spot without having enough time to think things over, you'll be familiar with that uncomfortable, dissatisfied sensation that often follows when you're not quite sure what you agreed to or whether you've made the right choice. This is the manipulator's favorite tactic to force you into complying with their schedule, and they'll hold you to your agreement. Try to back out of it, and they'll immediately lash out at you, painting you as the "bad guy" because you're backing out on your word. The most effective tactic to stem off this unwanted pressure is to say no to buy yourself some time repeatedly. Tell them firmly that you need time to think things over, and you don't appreciate being put on the spot like that. If they try to make you feel guilty by pretending to be upset or angered at your resistance, let them know you're sorry they feel that way, but you are still sticking to your answer, and you need time to think things over. When they try to bully or intimidate you, once again firmly but politely tell them that you don't appreciate being intimidated into making a decision. They need to respect your need to take some time. At the first sign that you might be onto what they're trying to do, the manipulator would usually retreat.

Avoid Them - The most straightforward way to stop manipulators is to avoid them in the first place. Of course, this is often easier said than done since sometimes these manipulators exist within your own immediate family. Since they're family, it can be hard to sever all ties with them completely, so the best thing you can do is avoid them. Do everything that you can to stay away from them where possible. During those few moments where they're unavoidable, such as family gatherings, for example, minimize your contact with them by surrounding yourself and keeping busy with the other non-toxic family members. They might not be entirely avoidable (unless you were to leave the company for a better job), so the best thing you can do is once again minimize the contact you have with them. Communicate through emails to avoid interacting with them directly, and when you do need to, try to get another colleague to come along with you as a witness of sorts. This leaves the manipulator with little chance of twisting their story or denying what they said.

Fire Back at Them with Questions - If there is one thing that manipulators avoid, it is having others discover what they're really up to. The minute you start firing back at them with probing questions each time they try to force you into meeting an unreasonable demand, flip it around back on them and probe them with questions they'll be reluctant to answer. Since their requests or statements will be unreasonable most of the time, it is an opportunity for you to let them know that you're fully aware of what they're trying to do. Put them on the spot by asking questions that include whether they believe this request is fair or reasonable and how this arrangement will benefit the two of you mutually. These questions will make them uncomfortable, and they won't answer them without revealing themselves. When they're dismissive of your questions, be firmer and keep pressing the issue, making it clear you expect them to answer. An effective way to get them to back off and stop putting so much pressure on you.

There's so much to remember and be mindful of in your dealings with the manipulator. However, there is one reminder that you shouldn't forget, and that is never to blame yourself or feel guilty that you were a victim. Making you feel that way is exactly what they want, but don't let them get inside your head. They're deceptive and conniving, willing to do many things that most people would not, and anyone could have easily become a victim just as much as you were. Just because they picked on you, it doesn't mean that there is anything wrong with you. We all have our strengths and weaknesses; it's part of the dynamic that makes us human. Blaming yourself is playing right into their hands, and if you are beating yourself up over it, don't do it.

Effectively Dealing with the Silent Treatment

Here's something you need to know about manipulators who use the silent treatment. They're emotionally stunted people who resort to this childish approach over choosing to have a mature conversation to resolve any kind of problem. They may look like adults, but their behavior reflects a childish, underlying personality beneath it. They're so used to getting what they want that they kick up a fuss when things don't go their way. Pretty much like what a child would do. Besides ignoring them and refusing to play their game (meaning groveling and begging for their forgiveness the way that they are hoping you would), here's what you can do to stomp on the manipulator's attempts at trying to abuse you with the silent treatment emotionally:

Point Out Their Behavior - They're not going to be used to people calling them out on their bad behavior, since most of the time, the general reaction that tends to follow the silent treatment is the victim continuously trying to reach out to them, asking them what's wrong and what they can do to make things better. Manipulators want to feel in control, and very rarely are they going to encounter someone who pushes back by saying, "I know what you're trying to do, and it's not going to work with me." Whenever they revert to the silent treatment to get you to submit, do the exact opposite. Let them know that you're not going to tolerate being emotionally abused with the silent treatment this way, and when they're ready to have a proper conversation about it, they can come and talk to you. If they choose to keep sulking and ignoring you, let them be, it is not your responsibility to try and fix a situation caused by their bad behavior. Eventually, which is often when they need you, they'll come around, and that's when you move onto the point below.

Discuss Their Behavior - Once they're done throwing their little temper tantrum and start behaving like an adult again, have a discussion with them about what happened. They'll do everything that they can to avoid the subject, but be persistent and let them know that you're not going just to sweep this under the rug. Talk to them about how abusive you through their behavior was (this will put them on the alert, worried about being discovered again), and how you see this affecting your relationship with them. They will try to turn things around and make it out to be your fault that they behaved this way because you were the one who angered them or upset them in the first place. When they do, shut them down and say while you do feel sorry that they felt that way, it was still no way to treat you when they could have chosen other ways of dealing with the issue. Make it clear that regardless of how they felt, silent treatment abuse was never the right approach to take. The manipulator will wake up when they realize that their maneuvers do not as easily fool you as they initially believed.

Don't Resort to Tit for Tat - Dealing with manipulators can be unbelievably frustrating. On several occasions, you may be tempted to give them a taste of their own medicine, use the same approach they are taking with you, and treat them the same way.

Chapter 3. Stages of a Relationship with a Covert Narcissist

A relationship with a narcissist doesn't have the natural flow and is characterized by stages absent in healthy relationships. The natural balance of giving and take is disrupted. Relationships with such individuals start with infatuation and idealization, only to end devaluation, rejection, and complete discard of narcissist's partner. In psychological and therapeutic practice, there are three main stages of a relationship with a narcissist: the idealization phase, devaluation, and discarding.

Idealization

During the idealization stage, the narcissist earns their target's trust by showing them affection, appreciation, praise, and adoration. They lift the other person, cheer for them, offer unlimited support, a shoulder to cry on, act as a friend in need, and a perfect lover who just knows how to make things right. This is called love bombing, and during this phase, narcissists aim to recreate the ideal relationship and earn the trust and loyalty of their targets.

Covert narcissists have a fluid identity that allows them to transform like a chameleon and adapt to any person they are to gain their respect and trust. They are perceptive, analytical and will investigate the target carefully to create the perfect scenario that gives them the green light to the phase of a relationship we will soon talk in the text. It is in a narcissist's interest to be liked, and so they create the persona that is likable as the only thing they care for is admiration. This first stage is about their target's identity to get the admiration they believe they deserve. The behavior almost resembles a teenager who desperately wants to fit in with a group of popular people, just to be popular and liked themselves. Emotional detachment and infertility allow them to reflect on the person they are with, quickly attaching their needs and wants to the other person—they are giving because they know it will be appreciated and make them likable. Needing acceptance and admiration from you, a narcissist will do anything to get it and go about it so smoothly that you will hardly notice they are mirroring who you are. In other words, they will do it covertly.

The love bombing is based on acts and words of adoration that are excessive and "too good to be true." The survivors of narcissistic abuse often say that the relationship with covert was like heaven in the beginning. "It was perfect." "It felt like a fairy tale." "Our relationship was ideal." "I thought I finally found someone who gets me." "They made me feel special." "They seemed like the person I have been waiting for all my life." "I thought I have finally found my soulmate." "We were the best couple." "We had so much in common." "Back then, I felt so lucky I found them." They identify how to target your weaknesses and use them to manipulate you, at this stage by earning your trust by building you up in those areas you feel insecure about. When love bombing, they will realize you and the relationship, make you feel very special and worthy of love, only to make you feel opposite at the two stages of the relationship.

It is very common for survivors of narcissistic abuse to say that they were very impressed by their covert having the same interests, lifestyle, and hobbies. A narcissist does detailed research on their targets and will spend time learning about and absorbing their interests, tastes, likes, and dislikes. While there is a natural incarnation, people have to be open to learning about interest people they like to have. In the light of a narcissistic personality disorder, this is not a result of curiosity, but a lack of identity and the desire to be so desperately liked and worshiped. Many love bomb others by taking care of their needs, giving them gifts, compliments, praise, taking them places, or being overly helpful even when there is no real help needed. This behavior has a certain level of pushiness, but because it seems genuine, the person who is being love-bombed perceives the narcissist as the nice person who just wants to love and care for them. Many of their former partners say they felt unexplainably uncomfortable for receiving so much attention and needing to return the affection or favors but couldn't recognize it as a red flag back then.

Ultimately, in the love-bombing stage of a relationship, the narcissist treats the other person as they were the same. Although it is never a conscious process in their mind, the people they are targeting are seen as an extension of themselves. In the beginning, this person is the extension of their praise-needy, self-important, "ideal" side of the personality, a boost to their ego that shows how valuable they are. The other person is a "replica" of himself or herself. They are a replica of that person, their interests, thoughts, and feelings. This process is called mirroring or projecting the aspects of self to the other person. However, it is a two-way street. At this first stage, a narcissist's target will feel very special, beautiful, respected for their talents, important or praiseworthy—which is exactly what narcissists think about themselves.

Everything they do, they need to be returned and in double or triple doses. If they do a lot of helpful things for you in the beginning stages of a relationship, rest assured they will require you to do little or big favors for them and make you feel guilty when you are not able to put a pause on your life and deliver what they need when they need it. The idealization phase is a base a narcissist builds to create a safe zone where they can be admired while gradually revealing their true selves as the relationship progresses. The paradox of this disorder is that the narcissist knows that connecting with other people is open, empathetic, and interested in the other person. Therefore, they use it to create an environment where they can be who they are—the empathetic, closed-off person who doesn't care about the other. The final goal is to make the target comfortable enough to refocus the relationship towards themselves gradually.

This stage, just like the other two, is as present in work and family environment as much as it in love relationships and friendships. For instance, covert narcissists are often praised and respected members of society, many of which are very involved with charity work or are in important positions. They care about their status and what others think of them, so naturally; many will opt for careers that allow them to be in the spotlight in one way or another. Covert colleagues and bosses will be the first ones to hop in to help you with tasks, help you get things done, and even take on your part of the job on themselves. This, however, lasts only during the first stage, when you get to know them. They appear agreeable, kind, generous, charismatic and everyone seems to love them. Remember, no matter what place they take in your life, there are always three stages of a relationship with the present. Don't be surprised that once the appreciation bombing phase is over, you get criticized, unappreciated for things you were once praised for, or if they take the credit for your ideas or give it to someone else. They want your full trust and give you praise and help whenever you need and don't need it, only to twist the reality and diminish your ambition, work drive, and health.

Devaluation

At this stage, little things they adored about you suddenly become flaws and something you are ashamed of. Once the relationship is established, and the covert has created a haven by gaining your loyalty and trust, they gradually start expressing their dissatisfaction with the relationship and you. Because they have first carefully analyzed your weaknesses and built you up, they will start using your fears and insecurities against you. Although never or rarely openly, they slowly diminish their target's self-confidence by planting the seeds of self-doubt, fear, and even self-hate in them. This happens periodically. It is hard to pinpoint and even harder to understand because it is done subtly and entwined with sporadic acts of love and kindness, especially at the beginning of this stage.

The trouble here is that a covert narcissist devalues their partners subtly and appears completely innocent in the process. Most often than not, this devaluation manifests in little things they don't do for you rather the things they say directly and openly, especially at the beginning of this stage. Because it is a covert narcissist we are talking about, this phase can revolve simply around them not acknowledging your needs, wants, and desires, showing less and less interest in your life and you as a person. They will not shout, be cruel in obvious ways, yell or say mean things. Instead, they will damage your self-esteem in little, subtle ways, turning to more serious manipulation techniques. Devaluation can go from little things like not replying to text messages, not calling when agreed upon, or prioritizing other people or things to give silent treatments, criticizing, nitpicking, or blaming others. The reason for devolution is to make them feel better about themselves because that is the level of emotional maturity the narcissist operates on.

This can manifest as falling from the number one worker to the average one, comparing or praising other employees who put in even less effort than you do. At the beginning of his career at the company, Richard was his boss's favorite employee, always prized for his ambition, problem-solving skills, and efficiency. It was his dream job, so he tried his best to put all his enthusiasm into it. However, as time went on, he could hear his boss complaining about the little mistakes he made in the prospects, the tidiness of his office, or his time-management. These were nothing new, but unlike before, where such tiny mistakes weren't recognized as major, which they are not, were now seen as Richard's lack of professionalism and capability to meet required criteria. He did extra hours and took on more responsibilities than he should prove his dedication, only for his boss to blame it on him for not finishing even more.

Chapter 4. Covert Emotional Manipulation Methods

In a manipulation method that is entirely based upon triggering emotions, it should come as no surprise that at the end of the day, there are nearly endless ways that you can go about manipulating the emotions of others. We will take a look at five different methods that can be used to toy with other people's emotions, allowing you to understand that you will need to use them in any way that may work best for you. We will be going over the use of fear, obligation, and guilt to keep people under your thumb with emotional blackmail. We will look at how you can play the victim, invalidate your target, gaslight, and use a love bombing method and devaluing. These will create emotions within the other person you can use to get exactly what you want or need to see.

Emotional Blackmail

Emotional blackmail is a common way that people can be controlled. When you do this, you are using the threat of either fear, obligation, or guilt to try to get everyone around you in line. Essentially, you will be relying on the fact that fear, obligation, and guilt are all incredible motivators. They can be used to trigger that motivation to make the negative emotions end through, making it a point to trigger them by failing to do what you wanted in the first place. Each of these works in their ways, but at the end of the day, they require you to have some sort of leverage over the other person that can directly be used to control them. That leverage will be what you use to trigger one of these responses.

Fear

When you are using fear, you need to have a credible way to make the other person feel afraid. You may use the fear of losing you. For example, you can threaten to break up with someone. You may use the fear of some sort of punishment or abuse. You may use the fear of just about anything to get someone moving and in line.

Obligation

This is most commonly used in relationships or amongst families. When you attempt to use an obligation to try to get someone working toward what you want them to do, you somehow make what you want them to do an obligation or responsibility of theirs, so they feel like they have no choice but to do so. Frequently, you see this in relationships in ways such as saying, "But you owe me after everything that I did for you!" This is meant to make the other person feel like they do have no choice in the matter—if they do not live up to your expectations, they are left feeling guilty and, therefore, responsible for what has happened or are left feeling like it is otherwise all their fault. Still, either way, it is a struggle for them.

Guilt

Finally, when you use guilt as a weapon, you are frequently telling the other person that it is their fault that things did not work out. You may say that you are now in a very tight or bad spot because of their inaction in doing something, or you may try to make it the other person's fault when something goes wrong. For example, if you need money for something, you could guilt the other person into paying for it by letting them know how badly you need it, but you cannot afford it. You may have been able to afford it just fine—but you will never let the other person know that. You may also try to put down the guilt in other contexts as well—perhaps you remind the other person that they are responsible for their children's safety, so they owe it to their children to buy the most expensive car they are approved for, even if it is going to be pushing their budget a bit more than they are comfortable doing. The guilt they would feel at not buying that car with more safety features is enough to push them toward making it a point to buy the other car instead, despite not wanting to initially.

Playing the Victim

Another common way to emotionally manipulate other people is to play the victim role. When you switch yourself into the victim role, you are essentially making it a point to make the other person feel guilty for whatever they have done. For example, you may be in a situation in which you have messed up somehow. Maybe you forgot to pay a bill, and your partner is now angry about the addition of a fee that would otherwise not have to be paid due to the bill being late at this point. You know that you are at fault, but do you want to take the fall and the blame? Most people would prefer to avoid that blame altogether, so what you have to do is figure out how to redirect somehow. You need to be no longer seen as the perpetrator or the one at fault, but rather to be seen as the victim of some sort of unfortunate circumstance.

When you can shift the attention in that way, you can then take back control. You can no longer be the one at fault, but rather the one who was victimized instead. Perhaps you do this by pointing out how you had tried to pay the bill and that you thought the bill was paid, so it must be a banking error. Maybe you bring up how, on the day that it was due to be paid, something extreme happened that prevented you from paying for said bill. Maybe you even try to reverse the situation to make your partner the one at fault instead.

When you reverse the situation, your partner is the one at fault. This is known as DARVO—Deny, attack, and reverse victim and offender. When you follow these steps, you can make sure that you remain the one that is pitied or seen as the victim in the situation, which then allows you to defend yourself.

Deny: you start by denying the claim somehow. You say that you did not forget what had happened, or you say that you did not avoid paying the bill for some reason. You are going to refute whatever claim has been thrown at you. You could very easily substitute not paying a bill for claims of abuse, for example, or any other fault, whether you have done it or not. Denying it is the first step in the process.

Attack: now, you need to shift the burden onto the other person. You may say that your partner was the one that was responsible for those bills, or you claim that your partner was the one that was abusive or toxic toward you instead. The task here is to put your partner or whoever you are talking to on the defensive—you want them to suddenly feel like they have to refute your claim instead of asserting their own, which allows you to remain shielded.

Reverse victim and offender: finally, in this last stage, you are sort of rewriting the narrative—you are making it clear that you did not cause the problem, but rather, you are the one that is now having to pay more in fees due to the other person's incompetency or whatever else you are blaming. At this point, you want to assert that the other person is the offender and that you are the victim in this particular situation. If you played your cards right, the other person would be so busy trying to prove that they are not, in fact, the ones at fault that they will not realize what you have done.

Invalidation

Another common method to mess with the emotions of someone else is to use invalidation. When you are doing this, you make the other person feel like they are at fault for some reason. You are making them feel like they cannot trust themselves, and then you are preying on that doubt. One such form of this will be gaslighting, which we will be looking at shortly.

When you are using invalidation, you are essentially always saying things to use plausible deniability when they do try to blame you or call you out for the way you are treating them or acting. For example, imagine that you hear someone trying to manipulate say that they have just done something good eventually. Perhaps they are happy about the job that they just got hired for. If you want to make them feel invalidated, you would then shrug it off and mention how you did something better. If they try to tell you that you are hurtful, you can deny this and say that you were just sharing your successes.

You can also invalidate people by constantly pointing out why they are wrong, how they are wrong, and why they should change up what they say or why they are saying it. You can also make snide jokes and sarcastic comments. When they say something about what you have said hurting their feelings, you can then deny it all together—you simply tell them that they are too sensitive and not to be so willing to be hurt over something that was not meant to be taken that way in the first place. When you do this, reminding the other person that you did not do anything that was intended to be hurtful, you make them feel wrong and invalidated. They are stuck, feeling like they cannot defend themselves without looking petty or too sensitive.

Gaslighting

Gaslighting is a very specific form of invalidation. When you are using gaslighting, you are intentionally trying to make the other person doubt their perceptions around them. They may tell you that you did something, and you deny it, saying they are wrong. They may eventually believe the narrative that you are trying to push, and they made a mistake somewhere along the line, and that they are entirely wrong.

Usually, you start small—you correct them about where things came from or where you found something. This does not have to be significant—it just has to plant the seed that they are mistaken regularly. Slowly, you will up the stakes—you will start to remind them that they were wrong about when they did something or if something happened in the first place. Over time, you will eventually plant the idea that they cannot get what is going on around them right. They will stop questioning you when you suggest something and instead look at how they are always wrong. They will not trust themselves, which means that you would be able to lie to their faces about something that just happened practically, and they would take your narrative over their own.

Chapter 5. Knowing Yourself

The key to being able to avoid manipulation is to know yourself. You will not be able to know yourself unless you experience failure in the world. Most people experience enough failure when they become adults to know how they deal with it and learn how to keep going. If you don't know yourself, you will repeatedly use people who don't care a lick about you. They are just more focused on their own goals. When you know yourself, you can know other people better. You will be able to tap into that voice that tells you this is not worth it, that you are being manipulated. If you know yourself, you are less vulnerable to deceit and lies.

This is because people are very self-repressed, and they don't learn about themselves. By not learning about yourself, you are opening yourself up to the worst of interactions and relationships. Relationships are shallower when you are like this. They lack depth and concentration. When you know yourself, you can analyze what is happening to you and other people. When you know yourself, you can protect yourself.

Analyzing people involves keeping knowledge of how we see the world and how we move to observe others. This is why knowing yourself is so important. It takes a lot of effort to understand how other people see you globally, cueing you into their behavior. One way to start this is to look at the Enneagram of personality and see what line up mostly with you. This can tell you about the drives you have in your personality that you might not even realize. When you are trying to find out what type of personality you are, you are engaging in a self-reflexive behavior that will have you become a better person. It will help you to know yourself, and your intuition will be increased as a part of this.

Another way to know oneself is to participate in the art of watching or listening to art. A movie can tell us the story of a world. It is a way by which we understand the world. Every time you speak, you tell a story, either in words or as you say them. This can help you realize your strengths and weaknesses.

When you are reading a great novel, you become immersed in that book, and you get to share a little bit of the writers' world in your imagination. The writer and reader create a continuum, wherein the writer's consciousness is being followed directly by another person. They say that literature is the art that most people can escape their world and get into another person's consciousness. You start to learn the characters, and you start to predict what they are in to do. Characters in the story can be compared to people you know in real life, and the book can give your ideas of how to behave and change the world through your actions. As you get into the story, you are experiencing a ride that is the most positive way of expressing ourselves. This is art. Art is a mysterious way that we participate in the world. Art has the power to incite wars and peace. It is a way to disturb people deeply, and you can keep them happy and calm. Art (we are talking here about the art with a big A, as to mean every category of art, from dance to film to sculpture) is a way that we are in the world that lets us start a feedback loop with the world, and it becomes a source of communication with the world and with others. This is a way that we can find solace and express ourselves to the world.

Art is also a way that we immortalize ourselves. Each human is subject to the lifespan that they are given on this planet, and when you realize when your life is going to end eventually, you start to realize that the world will move on without you. This means that you might be forgotten, at least according to our primal fear. So, we try to do things to counteract this. The most primal and animal way is to have children because then you'll live on in the world through the people who you have created to carry out their own goals and happiness in the world.

Having children is a simple way that people leave a legacy, and it is the ultimate creative act in the world. All other forms of art are underneath this one. That is because art comes from consciousness. That is why humans are not art. We are conscious, we have the power of gods, and when we create another person, we use our power as gods. We are also using the power of gods when we create art, but it is slightly lesser.

Art is a way that you can analyze yourself to deeper levels. Remember the Rorschach test, a way of analyzing people where we look at blobs of ink of paper and say whatever comes to mind first? Well, all art is sort of like that, as a creator and as a viewer. As a creator, when you are creating art, you are creating the ink blob. Sometimes it is very clear what the artist is talking about. When you look at a Norman Rockwell painting, you understand the scene that he has created because he is putting you right there in a scenario that you can recognize and understand. The artist often puts you in a place where you can't understand because you aren't meant to. This kind of art can help us explore what it feels like for other people to experience tarts o fat world's tarts. Abstract art is not about telling you things but rather gets you to think. Many people say that literature is how you can most experience another persons' consciousness, out of all of the art forms. Think about the best book you ever read. You were so into it that you couldn't put it down, and when you read it, you were nowhere else except in the world created by the writer. You were a citizen in his world, and there was nothing to do except to be there in the story and experience whatever was going on.

When you do this, you are experiencing a human mode called flow. Flow is when you are just in the moment, when you are only experiencing something that you are doing, like meditating, playing the piano, running, driving, or something else. It is a state of focus and a state of creativity.

To know yourself, you have to be able to experience the extremes of life. You must have been able to understand the anger and express it. You must know when you feel angry and understand what that feels like to you. You must be able to experience joy at the highest level, for this is an extreme human feat. You must be able to take deep pain and failure and also accept the beauty in life. You must immerse yourself in the book and then pay some bills that you have lying around, which is just menial work that you have to do. You have to deal with all sorts of things that are big and small, and none is less important. It might seem that the small stuff is less important, and in many ways, it is, but the details are something that you can be vigilant with, and they are ways for you to let yourself experience each part of life.

The number-one way to do this concretely every day and learn about you is journaling. You can journal every day but never write the same thing twice. Journaling doesn't have to be your homework. It can be fun, it can be creative, and it can be a way to release yourself from the shackles of what binds you.

When you write about yourself, you are looking at yourself through the lens of another person, or at least not through your own. By writing about yourself, you are also able to tell your story. Let's talk about both of these aspects of writing.

When you write about yourself, you get to look at yourself through your own eyes, but more objectively. Or at least, that's the hope. When you open up the journal and start writing about yourself, and it is all negative stuff, you should tell yourself that you have a problem there. When you are writing about yourself, try to be as subjective as possible. When you find that you cannot do this, it might mean that you are too much up in your head.

You see, we start to develop ideas and concepts about ourselves that may or may not be true. Even if they are true, they might not be so good to dwell on. Many people have problems with intrusive thoughts or automatic negative thoughts. If you are one of these people, just take your writing and see if you notice these thoughts in writing, and see if you can stop yourself and try to write out thoughts that are kinder and more accurate. By talking about ourselves more objectively, we can get more in touch with ourselves regarding our real desires, goals, and ways of living. When we are in our heads, we don't get a really good idea of our perceptions vs the world's perceptions around us. When we are all up in our heads about how we are, the world seems like a movie that we are starring in. When we write about our lives, you are writing a movie. An objective perspective will let you talk about yourself as a friend rather than yourself. You can start to think of this guy or girl as a person who is closer to the world than to your own experience, and when you do that, you reduce the number of feelings and thoughts that might get mixed up with the perspective. When you take out the emotions and thoughts and just go with the facts, you'll find that you can be fairer and more realistic about yourself.

Some people will find that they have self-esteem issues that they need to deal with. Others will be more on the side of narcissism, and they will need to learn about how to reduce their selfishness and start to think more about others. Telling a story is another big part of writing that is so beneficial to us. Writing a story can give you some narrative that will let you be expressive and real about your life. Telling the story tells you how you feel about yourself. You can see yourself as a character in a play or movie. What is the character like? Is he or she an antagonist or protagonist? What are the character's values, their role in life, and their role in the story?

Chapter 6. Psychological Tricks to Examine Human Beings

You must have heard it a lot of times already that communication is the key to everything—be it your relationships or your business deals. Everything is carefully balanced on how you choose to communicate with people, but it's easier said than done. It can be really hard to handle people the right way, but certain psychological tricks can come in handy. They help you examine the people around you to understand their motives, and they will also make your overall life much easier.

By now, you must have already understood that humans are not at all easy to understand, and they are quite complex. However, there are certain patterns in behavior that can be studied to make conclusions. If you think that examining someone can only be done through psychoanalysis and not otherwise, you are wrong because it can also be done through other tricks, which are relatively easier. Even if a person raises an eyebrow or stands in a particular manner, there is meaning to it, and this meaning, when deciphered, will help you understand that person.

I know what you must be wondering. It is just like any other skill you learn. Understanding and examining a human being is not any different. With time, as you keep practicing, you will notice that you have developed an inner intuition that will always guide you in the right direction. Whether you want to understand how you should approach your boss or in what way you should speak to please your client, all of those tactics can be mastered through some simple psychological tricks. Do you know who the top performers in a company are? They are not the ones who are the smartest in the room. They are the ones with the best people skills and know-how to communicate.

You simply need to practice every day to tune in and understand what every person is thinking or how they are as a person. If you want your relationship-building skills to improve, there are different ways to make educated guesses about people from now on.

Let us look at some of these tips and tricks, and I hope you can apply them to the person you meet.

Look Into Their Eyes

I have to say that looking into someone's eyes is the first and foremost trick that everyone should learn. Eyes are the doorway to the mind, and they convey much more than we can imagine. You will often come in situations where you do not particularly prefer the answer you got, and when that happens, you do not understand why things happened the way they did. You might have expected a different answer, and now that the opposite happened, you can't seem to figure out why. Sounds familiar? Well, then you are in luck here because looking into that person's eyes can get you the answer you are looking for. The first reaction that most people have in such a situation is that they ask the question again, but that is most likely to get you the same answer once again. You should look deep into that person's eyes and try to understand what you see. When you do that, the person is automatically going to feel as if they are cornered. In short, they will feel a bit of stress, and this stress itself will bring you a lot of answers. Most of the time, in such situations, the person tries to elaborate on why they said what they said.

Apart from the situation, I just explained, looking into someone's eyes will help you take a peek into their mind. If someone is trying to dismiss what you are saying or is not liking the conversation, you can make it out if you truly look into their eyes.

Now, let us go into some of the details. One of the first things you should keep in mind is to watch for any changes in the pupil's size. I am going to give you an example from a study that was published in the year 1965. It was conducted to show the difference in the pupil's size in response to the people (Eckhart H. Hess, 1965). The psychologists had produced semi-nude pictures belonging to both sexes to female and male participants. There was an increase in the size of the female participants' size when they saw men's pictures. Similarly, there was an increase in the size of the male participants' size when they saw women's pictures.

Subsequent studies were done by the same psychologists to find more information. Homosexual participants were included, and the same result was obtained. Their pupils increased in size when they saw pictures of men in semi-nude condition. Simultaneously, when pictures where mothers were coddling babies, were shown to women, their pupils dilated. So, do you see where this experiment is heading? It is not the only arousal depicted by pupils' dilation, but it also shows whether the information shown is interesting and relatable.

Now, let us move on to something much more complex—when you become an expert at reading the eyes, you can also determine whether a person is telling the truth or lying by simply looking at their eyes. In the year 2009, another study was conducted in which one group of participants did not steal, and the other had stolen $20 (Andrea K. Webb, 2009). Whether the participant had stolen the money or not, every one of them was asked to say the same thing that they had not stolen anything. The detection of a thief was possible when pupil dilation was examined for denying the theft. When the pupil dilation of both groups was compared, it was noticed that the ones who were lying witnessed an increase in pupil size, which was 1 mm more than those who did not commit the theft.

Another thing about the eyes that you should keep in mind is that when people close their eyes in the middle of a conversation, it is usually because there is some feeling that they are trying hard to bury inside themselves. It can also be that they are trying to hide from the chaos of the outside world. However, what you should remember is that closing the eyes does not necessarily mean that the person is afraid of you. It is quite the opposite. They might be finding you annoying, or something about the conversation is irritating them, which is why they want to shut you out. It makes them feel that even when you are in front of them, closing their eyes means that they can shut you out momentarily and not have to see you.

Find the Hot Buttons

If you want to understand someone and their motives, you have to find out more about their hot buttons. It starts with recognizing the hot buttons first. Hot buttons are people's pain points, and they help you understand what they are thinking. The best way to recognize these points is to ask the right questions, and for that, the first step is to build a rapport and a good bond with the person. In short, you have to be a good listener first and a small mouth.

Whenever you want to know more about a person, the trick is to ask questions that give the person room to answer away. These are called open-ended questions. Asking questions whose obvious answers are yes or no is not going to help you here. Questions that require the person to speak about them, their challenges, and their strengths are what you need. Another way to approach this situation is to talk to the person and share stories from your own life where you have done something helpful for other people. Most of the time, you will find people telling you that they have been facing something similar in their life, and this conversation will help you a lot. For starters, it will help you to understand what this person truly needs.

One of the first mistakes that people make is that they think not everyone has triggered, but you are wrong here—everyone has them. The only difference is that some people are good at hiding their triggers. If it is of any help, I am going to give you examples of some of the most common hot buttons that people have:

Fear

I am mentioning fear at the beginning of this list because it is the most powerful hot button. Two of the most common situations, when fear shows itself as a hot button in a person, are avoiding pain or trying to seek pleasure. However, you also have to keep in mind that fear does not act in the same way for everyone. What you fear in life might not be the same for someone else and vice-versa. Fear depends on the experiences that people have in their lives. If you notice this hot button in the person, you have to use it to your benefit. Give them a solution that removes their fear, and this option should eliminate all doubts.

Anger

Anger is something we all experience in our daily lives, and to be honest, quite frequently. However, what is important here is that you have to notice how someone is reacting to this emotion and how it affects their ability to form decisions. If there are any choices that you are looking to change, then you have to keep an eye on how anger is influencing those choices in the person. But if you want to use this hot button for your benefits, the first thing that you should do is try and understand it.

Greed

We make the mistake of thinking that only some people are capable of greed. But no, greed is present in some form in all of us. The degree of greed in a person varies, and yet, it is still there. Greed is mostly about a fear that you won't get anything out of a situation and that you will be left lonely. This gives rise to the thought that no one can take things from you when you have everything. This makes people go to great lengths just because they are looking for approval and acceptance.

Chapter 7. Basic Body Language Signals

Now that you are aware of the "what" and the "why" of body language, let's get into the "how." How can we start to pick up on people's body language? What different secrets are waiting to be discovered within the way that somebody holds their body? It's not easy to know exactly what somebody is trying to tell us, but the more we focus and study these aspects, the easier it will be to get what people are trying to say.

Closed-Off Body Language

Everybody has their reason for wanting to get to know what different body language signals mean. Suppose you are an individual who plans to have closer relationships with people and more successful business interactions. In that case, we must understand what closed-off body language looks like.

Often, when we might be interacting with somebody, the other person could feel a little anxious or reserved because they don't want to share certain parts of their life. While they might continue to talk to you, you could start to pick up how they might be closed off from you so that you can better understand whether or not they want to be in this active conversation or if they're trying to be a little bit more avoidant.

With the use of an arm cross, you can also notice that they might be crossing their legs in the same instance. Because we are primates and animals in general, we focus on self-preservation.

This means that we will often protect ourselves and our bodies no matter what we might be feeling at any certain moment.

What you also have to understand is that there are certain times when we might simply be cold. It's not in a metaphorical sense. We can merely experience times where the temperature is low, and we want to warm ourselves up.

There is another important area we can look at when deciding whether somebody is being closed off or if they are just the type of person who is a little bit more reserved. You can take notice of the tension in their mouths.

Those who are closed off and who do not want to be open with you will have stiff shoulders and flexed muscles. If somebody is cold, they might have little self-soothing habits they're doing, such as touching their arms a little bit or even rubbing their hands together.

When somebody is a little bit more open, then they'll keep their arms to the side and their chest exposed to you. This is because they are not afraid of what you might do to them. When somebody feels comfortable and confident within a situation, they won't exhibit the easily identifiable closed-off body language signals.

Remember, the reason that someone might close themselves off is not necessarily because they are afraid of the other person. Still, rather they could do this is because sometimes they just want to hide or have some other generalized anxiety within that moment and simply do not wish to allow the other person to see what we are doing.

If you want to make somebody with closed-off body language a little more open, you can begin to mirror their behavior. This means that you can mimic how they're closed off and holding their bodies in one instance, and then as they become more comfortable with, you switch into a little bit more of an open body language.

Preening and Repeating

One thing that many humans and other animals frequently do is they will go through an act of preening. Preening is when we are subconsciously cleaning and preparing ourselves for other people. Acts of preening include fixing up somebody's hair. Maybe they are playing with their hair by pulling stray hairs out or smoothing it down as they sit there and talk to you. They might run their fingers through their hair, move it to the side, throw it up in a ponytail, or do anything else that will indicate that they are fixing their hair from a state of what it was to state where it's a little bit cleaner and more presentable. This could also be seen through how we might pick ourselves while we are talking to other people. Some people pick at mini scabs on their faces. They might also be picking at their chapped lips or fidgeting with their hands and picking at the cuticles around their fingernails.

Perhaps they are going through short periods of scratching as well. Scratching isn't always a preening way and can sometimes display that the person is itchy or nervous. Sometimes we scratch ourselves when we're nervous because it feels as though we might be doing some active preening on a smaller scale.

Scratching yourself is a way to heal, but it's something that feels good and alleviates some of the pain or tension we might be feeling from different discomforts in our body.

Think of how dogs need to wear cones after surgery or go through another experience where they might have a wound or sore. Though it might not itch all the time, they might still try to scratch it as often as possible. The dog doesn't realize that this can make things worse; they do it because it's a natural feeling we have inside ourselves to alleviate some of the wound's discomfort.

This feeling gets twisted around in our brains, and we'll do the same kind of action when we're feeling nervous or anxious. It's a form of preening in some instances, but it could also simply indicate that the person is feeling uncomfortable or uneasy. Preening is also seen in how we might pamper ourselves or prep our looks using different products or makeup. Many individuals often associate trimming with women trying to be a little more romantic or flirtatious. The thing that we have to remember about preening is that it doesn't mean that another woman is attracted to you and trying to get your attention. She could only be feeling insecure and want to make herself feel better.

Preening in front of other people can also indicate that there is some form of competition. For example, suppose a woman chose to go into the women's restroom where it's a little bit busier and freshen up her makeup in front of other people. In that case, some might take this as a subconscious signal that she's letting others know that she is the top competition. She's fixing herself up and making sure that those around her know just how beautiful or powerful she might be. Preening is also seen in how we can sometimes clean up the area around us or rub imaginary lint off our bodies when talking to other people.

We go through some acts of preening because we want to feel more confident with our appearance, or we might be showing our worth through our attraction from other people.

If somebody is presenting in front of you, then it could be a sign of insecurity. It could also be a sign that they are making themselves more desirable for you.

Understanding the context of the situation will help you determine the intention of their preening. We also have to consider the repetition movements that somebody is using in their body language. Specific individuals might do the same kind of move over and over again. That could be somebody trying to persuade you, and they want to reiterate a point so that you are more likely to be convinced by the things they're sharing.

This can also be seen in how people are preening if somebody is constantly trimming while in front of you, it could be a sign that they are simply anxious. For example, you might have a friend who's always picking and touching her hair. Maybe she is a little bit more insecure. She might put a high weight on her hair because she identifies herself with these looks.

It's vital to notice repetition in how people use their body language to understand their intention better.

Mirroring Body and Speech

Mirroring body language is something that we have already touched on; however, let's take a more in-depth look into why we reflect and how we can use it to help other people connect with us further. Mirroring is the act of mimicking somebody else's body language. It's as if you are a mirror, and you pick up how they're moving and doing that yourself.

Mirroring happens from the moment we're born. We start to mimic the emotions and facial expressions of the people who raise us because we learn how to feel. For example, if you walked up to any baby between six months and 12 months old and started smiling at them, there's an excellent chance they're going to smile back. They have no idea why they're smiling, but they're going to do it because somebody else is showing them this act.

Mirroring is very normal. If you notice somebody mirroring you, that's not necessarily a sign that they're trying to control you. However, mirroring can be used as a tactic to get closer to somebody. Mirroring can be a way to connect with somebody and let them know that they are in a safe and comfortable space

Mirroring frequently happens subconsciously as a way to connect with other people. It helps remind us that we are not alone and that we are similar to others. In a world where we can sometimes feel like an outcast, we must focus on looking for ways to connect with others. Mirroring can also be very influential. If you are in a situation where you want to help somebody get into a different state, you can start by mirroring them.

For example, let's say that you're talking to a friend and they are having an awful day. They're feeling down about themselves; nothing seems to be going right; they're upset, and they're on the verge of tears. As a good friend, you want to help cheer them up; you want to better mood. So, you would start by mirroring the position that they're in at that moment. They might be hunched over with their arms around their legs, looking down and feeling sad. You don't want to do the same position because that's too obvious; however, you can hunch over as well. Let your arms hang or rest on the top of your knees and maybe tilt your head to the side as you talk to them.

You're letting them know that their feelings are valid and that they aren't alone. You're there to support them, and you're going to help work through these emotions with them. After you mirror their body language and pick up on this, you can change their body language after a few moments and sit like this and let them spill their feelings; maybe you sit up straight.

Chapter 8. Strengthen or Change the Views of Others

If you say anything that is consonant with my views, I, of course, agree with you. The fact is that it is easier to argue an already established opinion than to acquire a new one. Besides, every time you formulate a belief to yourself, it is a little more firmly fixed in your brain. If you tell others about it, it becomes almost impossible for the brain to restructure.

Therefore, wanting to influence a person, try to find out exactly his convictions. If your neighbor thinks that you bake the most delicious cakes in the city and you would like to support this opinion in every way, try to make her conviction even stronger: ask her to tell others about your cakes, preferably to the widest possible range of people. Moreover, even better if she puts out a photo of pastries with praise on Instagram for all her friends. Publishing our views is the most powerful way to convince ourselves that we think so. It does not matter that the judgment was initially not very well thought out —if we wrote it down and shared it with others, it would take a lot of effort to take our words back. Therefore, the keyboard or pen and the public who can read are your best helpers when you need to strengthen someone's rather weak beliefs: for example, that you are the best or that communism is great. (Believe it or not, but this was used by Chinese military leaders during the Korean War, forcing American prisoners of war to write and then read aloud that they renounced capitalism and became true radical socialists. It led to a change of political views: many soldiers returned to the US as Communists. However, the Chinese army overlooked the fact that similar beliefs were used in the United States, so soon, the former prisoners had turned back to capitalism.)

If in this way, you manage to strengthen the person in his views, he will defend them. Even if they try to convince him otherwise, he will persist—just to not look like an idiot, spreading unsubstantiated opinions.

And what if you need not back up the conviction but form it? If the neighbor does not like your cakes, it is necessary to prepare the ground for her to change her mind. Then make sure she doesn't do any of the above. Let him keep his opinion with him and not tell anyone about him. Do not ask what she thinks of her cakes—because then she will be even more convinced that she is right. The less chance she has of expressing her views, the more chances you have to change them. Act as Chinese commanders (although this appeal does not apply to other situations): bring to her the opinion you need—and in full compliance with covert reception, show that there are quite a few people who think the same way.

The neighbor will then be easier to abandon their former weakly expressed opinions and join the "wise" majority's point of view.

Influencing Opinion, Distracting Attention

I suspect that everyone who has an adoring sports partner in life often uses this feature for their good. They know that when a match is broadcast over the radio, the partner loses the ability to hear something else. This phenomenon has deeper roots than adherence to the colors of the local football club. Here we discuss the redistribution of brain resources, which cannot support several active states' functions.

For example, suppose you want to convince your partner that it is very different from his opinion. In that case, it is very useful to distract him from other impressions while you present him with your argument.

It is much easier to incline to your opinion a person who is watching TV while you are talking to him—even if the sound is muted. After all, the interlocutor's brain must process information coming from you and visual information (a football match). So, he can no longer allocate sufficient resources for the search for weighty counter-arguments. Similarly, it is much easier to convince you to buy many things on Amazon.com if you, while wandering around the site, simultaneously talk on the phone.

This conclusion is confirmed time after time. A diffuse consciousness (that is, a brain that performs several operations at once) is easier to manipulate and subject it to changes than when it is focused on one thing.

Dispelling the attention is not difficult. If you make a presentation in your company, you put a model next to you; you will notice that you can get any nonsense out of your audience. You can do the same as in the example with the TV—wait until the one you want to convince of your rightness is distracted by something, and at that moment strike.

However, such distracting techniques are not always convenient to apply in practice. If a distracting object is too noticeable, for example, if only models are wearing swimming trunks from a swimsuit, you risk that the rest will not be up to you. As a result, you will not receive any objections or approval. Meanwhile, there are subtler ways to dispel attention than just turning on the TV or simultaneously talking on the phone. Strictly speaking, it is enough to use random words. When we hear something different than we expected to hear, the brain seems to be dramatically slowing down at full speed and thinks "Stop, what else is that?"

Consider an example. If we discuss the price with you, then there are certain rules by which this discussion is based. Among other things, it usually sounds like the word "crowns." If you suddenly declare that the thing you want to sell is nine thousand cents (instead of ninety dollars, as I expected to hear), my thought will turn off for a moment from the well-groomed road. At this second, you will have the opportunity to turn my desire to buy something in the right direction—for example, saying: "It's fabulously cheap!" Confirmed by experiment: several researchers, selling Christmas cards, almost doubled sales when they started calling prices cents instead of dollars.

Pay attention: it is not enough just to knock the client's thoughts off the beaten path; thus, you only create a "window" in which you can influence the brain. For the reception to work, you must embed your message into the interlocutor's mind about how good or cheap a certain product is or how this person needs it. Researchers went up sales only when they began to pronounce the phrase "This is very cheap!" indicating their postcards' price in the cent. (When they called the price in dollars, nothing happened, no matter how much they claimed that the postcards were cheap.) The man who sold mini-muffins managed to increase sales, distracting customers with the unusual word "half-muffins," followed by the phrase that formed the conviction "They are amazingly delicious!"

Regardless of whether you use a sophisticated version, uttering unusual words, or are discussing plans for a vacation with might and main, with a person immersed in Dark Souls 2, dispersing attention, in any case, is a great way to make others more pliable.

It remains only to tell them what opinion they should hold.

Form "Others" About Them

You may not believe me, but your idea of yourself is largely based on what others say about you. The most famous experiment on this topic was conducted in one of the schools, where pupils of one class were told that their intelligence level was higher than of other children. Delighted with this news, the children immediately began to show much better results in the controls.

For example, this means that you can change your cousin's identity by treating her as if she has already become what you want her to be. With this technique's help, you can influence those around you, so that they correspond to your ideas and act as you need. Perhaps you want to convince someone to vote for your party. Join your church community. Get undressed already on the first date. Or just support your proposal at a workshop on Monday. Think about what type of personality is required to perform such an action. Then, make it clear to the one you have chosen to target that he is the carrier of precisely such value orientations.

It may seem difficult at first glance, and people will resist—they probably have some idea of what they are. However, nothing is easier. For example, a colleague suggests taking a test on personality traits, and then, showing him mysterious figures that are difficult to interpret, explain that he is conservative and prefers well-tested solutions (and therefore should be captivated by your offer). Or—that he is a man of an adventurous warehouse and has nothing against a certain amount of risk (if you need such a turn). Just forget to speak convincingly, leaving no reason to doubt your words.

However, in reality, there is no need to go so far and carry out pseudo-diagnostics. It is enough to talk about what your partner is doing in everyday life and describe his actions, taking into account the value orientations currently beneficial. "Oh, you chose a new sort of ice cream? So it seems to you to always try new things." "You can make an adventure out of everything." "It is very typical for you always to take risks." If a colleague hears several times that his actions indicate a propensity to take risks, he will begin to perceive himself as an adventurous person. He will then easily decide to press the big red button when you ask him about it (or what other actions you have to incline him).

If you need to encourage belonging to a different type of personality, emphasize its inherent qualities. Do you want a colleague to feel like a person with developed empathy? In this case, you ask "You took me coffee too? You, like anybody, always think of others." Alternatively, do you need strategic thinking? Then you will say, "An excellent thought is to drink something cold when it is so hot outside. It is noticeable that you are used to planning everything." When a colleague does something that does not fit the type of personality that you want to encourage, you will, of course, just keep silent.

You do not need much effort to make the desired changes. Secret advice for dating in a bar: First, make a woman interested in you feel like an adventurer—ask her to tell you about the various difficult situations she has been in, and then ask her to show you how much she likes to take risks. Between us, it is much faster and cheaper than to treat her to drinks at the bar.

Chapter 9. The Art of Persuasion

Persuasion, as an art, should be subtle and unnoticed. Less forceful than manipulation, more palatable than coercion, persuasion carries the assumption that those persuaded act out of their own 'fully informed' will and usually in a way that works towards the embitterment of all involved. This is not necessarily the case. However, framing an idea in an altruistic way of thinking is a good place to start. The following methods of persuasion are focused on being passive in our persuasion. We wait for the right time, consider their feelings, values, and standpoints. These tactics complement and support each other to create a practically impossible strategy to see through. So, they cannot be directly argued against or attacked with violating socially agreed-upon rules of conduct.

Using an honorable cause is a great way to get someone's attention. Still, an honorable cause alone is rarely enough to convert others to your way of thinking. To truly convert them, we must shift their focus away from the cause to their self-interest. Linking a great cause to the self-interest of listeners is an overwhelmingly powerful motivator. Once the listener begins to think about what they may get out of modifying their opinions or reassessing their loyalties, the cage door is closed.

As a rule, anyone can be persuaded of anything providing the timing, approach, and context are correct, but there are limitations such as time constraints. Before any attempt at persuasion, analyze the context of the situation as a whole and devise an acceptable approach based around the current underlying mood or general atmosphere, otherwise known as the emotional 'flow' of the situation. Do not go against the flow of the situation. Instead, use the emotional flow to your advantage. Frame your ideas as exciting when people are optimistic and as safe and pre-emptive in times of reflection. Going with the flow in this way allows you to siphon the already existing emotions in the room directly into your initiative. This method is ultimately more effective than simply trying to change the conversation topic to serve your purpose.

Timing is another pivotal factor when persuading others. The time of day greatly affects the expected desires of any particular person. For example, if we try to corner someone at work at 4 pm on a Friday, all they can think about is likely leaving work for the weekend, and so a large part of their brain will have already left the building. This could work to our advantage or against it depending on the goal. The timing of an approach extends beyond hours and days to weeks, months, and years. The longer we can plan, the greater our overall chances of success.

Identify those who are 'on the fence' or easy to influence and concentrate your efforts on these individuals in the same way politicians focus on 'swing' voters.

Most people are their own worst enemy, give them enough rope, and they will only be too happy to tie the noose. Ask questions that get people talking, and they will quickly voice opinions and values that can then be mirrored back at them in the present or used at a date to obtain their consent. Being cordial will cause people to open up to you. They will provide the information needed to devise an approach that speaks directly to their personally held beliefs and values. At that point, they will be powerless to refuse you or refute your way of thinking.

Do's and Don'ts of Arguments

We should be able to avoid most conflicts through clever maneuvering and planning. Still, there will be times when unpredictable people and events catch us off guard and are forced to either publicly or privately defend our position. By not instigating such situations, we automatically begin in a position of power from which we can choose exactly how to respond and set the tone for the rest of the interaction. If someone is attempting to start an argument or become abusive, it is likely caused by uncontrolled emotions, which implies that they have not planned. There are many ways to use this to your convenience, from passively listening (to obtain ammo) to deliberate provocation (to cause someone to lose their temper). From simple distraction to appealing to values, all have their benefits. However, some methods, such as baiting someone into a temper tantrum, will not win over your opponent and should only be used when attempting to influence the audience and as a last resort. The tips include actions and behaviors that should be avoided due to blatant nature and their futility, and the detrimental effect on influence and persuasion.

Do's

Keep Cool

It's easy to become caught up in a passionate moment or feel frustrated when faced with an argumentative and unreasonable individual. However, even a momentary lapse in composure can set us back massively, and it also gives those with an eye an opening to exploit. We do not need to restrain ourselves to the point that we are far removed; a little emotion helps keep the thought process flowing. It is a matter of balance; we must place ourselves somewhere between stoicism and enthusiasm without emotionally engaging any other individual or their point of opinion. Do not resist others' arguments, seek to augment them to your purpose by playing the long game, always be aware of the end goal, and remember that losing your temper is a sign of powerlessness.

Use Slick One-Liners Whenever Possible

Cleverly placed, hard-hitting one-liners can completely throw a person's chain of thought. A smart cliché or witty observation can completely demotivate an opponent for a few seconds, enough time for you to take control of the interaction. These seemingly spontaneous and intelligent interjections need not always make clear sense but sound reasonably sincere. You do not want to be seen as a heckler needlessly interrupting the flow of an otherwise relevant conversation. Here are a few of my favorite examples:

- Don't you think this will come back to bite us?
- Right or wrong, it's still beside the point.
- But what does that mean in the real world?
- What exactly are the parameters?
- You seem defensive.
- You're comparing oranges and apples.
- What research did you do?
- Use tactical contradiction.

When discussing matters in front of an audience, it is possible to convert those who are still undecided by dissecting and contradicting your opponent's proposal's specific points. By contradicting them, we have an opportunity to discredit their entire initiative. Even the 'airtight' points can be undermined through the association with premises that can be proved faulty or, even better, foolish. Don't be afraid of a little humor bordering on the theatrical. The audience will enjoy it; however, take care not to get carried away and become disruptive to proceedings.

Make an Appeal

From time to time, you will find yourself in a situation where you have exhausted your logic, expertise, and powers of persuasion. When this happens, it is no doubt since we missed a step along the way, leaving the listener/audience room for critical thinking. It is almost impossible to reverse engineer the interaction and start over immediately and mush in the same way that it is easier to win a new chess game than to recover one after a few poorly considered moves. In these cases, we can appeal to higher values, which will buy us valuable thinking time and also strengthen our position, so that we can then reapproach the issues from a slightly different angle by following up with some questions like:

- "Don't you think that this would make things safer for everyone involved?"

- "Shouldn't we be working together on this?"

- "Yes, but what kind of world do we want to leave for our children?"

- Practice pinpoint listening skills

People get emotional when they speak, and because of this, they make slip-ups, huge ones. Many people are terrified of speaking in front of others, and those who are not afraid of public oration are often overly confident in either themselves or their message. By intently listening to someone, we will at once be aware of their emotions. We can choose to 'pump' these emotions with questions directed to either excite or annoy. At this point, by pretending that you will concede a good point if only they see your point of view, they are likely to openly agree with you. The instant they do, undermine or contradict their point or objective. This simple 'bait and switch' technique will leave the opposition annoyed and confused, allowing you to take control and move on to other issues in the assumption that you have won this time. The people present will assume the same, and when the opposition sense this, they will internally admit defeat rather than go against the group consensus.

Play Devils' Advocate

By playing the part of the Devil's advocate, we can infuriate our opponent, prodding them until they lose their composure and the debate. Playing Devil's advocate consists of gently arguing against and questioning an idea relentlessly, even if we secretly agree with the point being made. It is a tactic that can also be used on your ideas. Question yourself in the way that you believe an incessantly annoying skeptic would and bolster the foundation of your position, and find better ways to protect and strengthen it. Doing so builds resistance to the negative comments, needless questioning, and others' behavior, which so often drains many of us of our creative juices and sometimes even confidence. When playing Devil's advocate to annoy an opponent, do so with a hint of ridicule and ask questions that severely stretch the premise of your opponent's position until the distortion causes it to appear absurd.

Don'ts

Indulge Distractions

Skeptics, disbelievers, and dissenters will often try to distract you with phoney and half-hearted arguments, and the truly argumentative may even attempt to push extreme examples of your ideas to distort them so that they seem ridicules or even reckless in the hopes of either redirecting your argument or causing you to lose your composure. Avoiding such distractions is not always easy, especially those that carry an emotional edge, but by being firm and focused, you can avoid deviations like digressions and subject changes. Resist the urge to dismiss or stifle others. Allowing others to opine is essential in so many ways. Thank them for their valued input, and Segway through some connection or other back to your original point, ideally using the interjection to strengthen your own ideas.

Make Personal Attacks

Lowering yourself and making personal attacks won't win advocates or arguments. You won't convert a person you've just offended, and anyone else present, will automatically assume that your ideas, as well as your integrity, lack substance.

Chapter 10. Influence Without Manipulation

Of course, not all social influence has to be manipulative either. There are several different ways that you can engage in influencing other people without ever having to step into the realm of manipulation if you would prefer to avoid it. These methods are largely more ethical and are meant to be beneficial to the other person, so you are not only taking advantage of another person for your benefit.

Influence can be particularly useful in situations that are not suitable for manipulation or when manipulation would likely violate any contracts or job descriptions you have now. Overall, you can think of many of the persuasive methods that will be here as the ethical, work-appropriate techniques that can be used without losing a license to practice medicine, sell a product, or practice law.

Principles of Persuasion

The principles of persuasion refer to a set of six different techniques that people find inherently persuasive. Using these persuasion principles, you can convince people to do things legitimately and honestly simply by appealing to one of six different principles. Of course, using any of these is not a guarantee for success, but rather it ups your chances of naturally convincing the other person to do whatever it is you are requesting of them. The six principles of persuasion are reciprocity, likability, authority, social proof, scarcity, consistency, and commitment.

Reciprocity

Reciprocity refers to the idea that people naturally want to return favors after they have had one done for them. Think of the feeling of obligation you may get when someone gives you a birthday present—you feel the need to return the favor when the other person's birthday rolls around. This is for a specific reason: you are convinced through reciprocity. This sort of nature's failsafe to the selfless behavior that humans have developed throughout evolution. With reciprocity, humans feel the need to return the favor whenever anyone helps them in any way.

Good, strong leaders recognize reciprocity as an inherent way the human mind works, and they will frequently bank on it—this is why you will see people ask, "What can I do for you?" when you come in somewhere. They are making it clear that they are interested in helping you, and hopefully, in return, you will help them as well. Good, emotionally intelligent leaders will almost always ask what they can do to help someone else before they ever ask the favor they had in mind. You can do this as well—offer to do something for someone. They will think that you are doing so out of the goodness of your heart. You may be, at least in part, but you will still have an ulterior motive. You can then ask the other person for a favor when you need it. For example, if you need to have your shift changed for a concert you want to attend in two months, you may volunteer the following time one of your coworker's mentions needing time off and needing a shift covered to get it approved. Your coworker then will probably offer to do something if he can repay you, at which point you can mention that you need your shift covered for the concert you want to go to, and your coworker agrees to do so. Now, you are left satisfied because your shift is covered, and you were not required to use manipulation to make it happen.

Likability

Likability refers to the fact that people naturally are more inclined to be persuaded when they like the person doing the persuading. After all, would you rather do a favor for your spouse, who you presumably love, or that coworker that you cannot stand? The answer is almost definitely that you would rather do something for your spouse, and the biggest reason for that is because you like your spouse.

Studies have shown that people are more likely to reach agreements in negotiations when all members take a moment to introduce themselves with some small tidbit of information about themselves that makes them more relatable. The biggest reason for this is because they become relatable, and when you relate to someone, you are more likely to want to come up with a compromise with them because you are more likely to feel empathetic toward them.

Luckily, there are three surefire ways to establish yourself as likable, even if your interaction with someone is relatively short. You will only need to take a few moments to do three simple things. You must first make yourself relatable, such as offering a small detail about yourself into the conversation naturally. Following, you should offer some sort of honest compliment to the other person. Lastly, you need to establish yourself as willing to cooperate to reach the same goal, effectively creating a team mentality. These three things can be the difference between landing that sale at work or failing to close.

Authority

People most often are willing to respect authority. They are usually willing to listen to someone who has established himself as an authority. For that reason, those viewed as authority figures are typically seen as more persuasive than those who are not. After all, you are more likely to listen to your dentist about how to save that tooth than the random cashier at the grocery store. This is due to your inherent bias that the dentist is more knowledgeable about dentistry than the cashier, and you are likely right. However, it is possible (and highly unlikely) that your cashier did go to school for dentistry.

When you want to make yourself an authority, you want to clarify that you know what you are talking about. You can do so by displaying your diplomas and other licenses you may have acquired during your career in your office. You can display awards that show just how good at your job you are. You could try including your credentials on your name placard on your desk or nametag. You could even have a secretary whose job is to sing your praises when answering the phone or greeting prospective clients. Suppose all of that is impractical with your job. In that case, there are other methods you can utilize as well—you can drop hints toward your experience in whatever topic you are discussing in a way that is natural with the client, such as mentioning that when you studied business back in graduate school, you learned certain concepts relevant to the conversation you are having. Simply dropping your experience in conversation makes it clearer that you do have some sort of experience, and therefore, your judgment should be trusted.

Social Proof

Social proof refers to the fact that people are largely more influenced by their peers than simply being told what to do for no real reason. This is essentially utilizing peer pressure to control someone else or recognizing that peer pressure principles are relevant to social interactions. For example, people are more likely to go along with their peers' behaviors than when they feel out of their element.

This can be used in manipulation and persuasion—you can hint that other people in a similar position made a choice similar to whatever you want the other person to do. For example, suppose you want to sell a mother of three children a car. In that case, you may point out that many of the parents that you sell to in the same boat as the mother repeatedly buy a minivan or SUV for the extra space for supplies for sports and extracurricular activities or even just to make up for the fact that children grow and may even outgrow a smaller car, feeling completely cramped if they do not have a third row to spread back toward. The mother may feel pressured as you mention this and be a bit more inclined to defer to what other people are doing simply because she was unsure anyway, and if other people are doing it, it likely works well.

Scarcity

The principle of scarcity is little more than supply and demand—people think that scarce things are more valuable simply because they are not as easily attained. With that in mind, you can make something seem more desirable or valuable simply by creating an artificial scarcity of the item. Companies do this frequently—you will see companies with business models that surround selling seasonal or limited time only items, and they draw out massive amounts of attention simply because everyone wants to get their hands on that new limited edition item, or they have been dying for that seasonal drink for months now. They are thrilled that it is finally available again.

When you want to use scarcity to control someone else, you can do so simply by making yourself scarce. Particularly in relationships, you see this utilized in one partner threatening to break up with the other, making it clear that their presence and commitment to the relationship is not guaranteed. If the other person cannot figure out what they are doing, then the person creating the request is willing to walk away altogether.

Consistency and Commitment

The last of the principles of persuasion is consistency and commitment. This refers to the fact that humans naturally value consistency. The easiest way to get that consistency is through commitments meant to motivate the individual to go through with what was committed to becoming consistent simply. For example, someone who has committed to doing something for you will likely follow through because with commitment comes obligation, and failing at obligations begets guilt, which most people want to avoid. If you want someone to do something, you must first start with a small commitment. It does not have to be particularly significant—even asking to borrow a pen would start this process. When that first commitment has been made, the individual is already in the mindset to continue saying yes, enabling you to continue asking for whatever you need. You can then attempt to get the other person to do something else, and you are somewhat more likely to get them to agree if you have already asked them to do something that they agreed to do.

Ethos, Pathos, Logos

Alongside the principles of persuasion, there is also the theory of ethos, pathos, and logos—three Greek words refer to appeals to different aspects of life to convince other people. When using these, you are essentially creating arguments in which you convince or compel someone to agree to do something because your argument is simply too compelling to deny.

Ethos

Ethos means ethics—it refers to appeals to ethical or moral duties. When you make an argument rooted in ethos, you are arguing for ethics. You are making it a point to spell out exactly why it is important to do things a certain way to avoid violating any inherent values of right vs wrong.

Chapter 11. Escape or Die

You may not die in the sense that your life will end, although that is a very real possibility. However, your freedom is sure to die. Your happiness will die. Your sanity will die. You will suffer a fate that is worse than death. If you were dead, you would be at peace. You would not have to suffer the endless misery that comes with being stuck in a manipulative situation. Instead, your body lives, but your spirit does not. You are trapped in an invisible prison, forced to suffer each day without the promise of ever getting free.

Of course, literal death is a tragic but very real possibility as well. At least three women each day are killed in the USA due to being in an abusive relationship. Countless more choose to end their own lives as it is the only escape from their torment that their broken mind allows them to see.

It doesn't have to come to this. There are several ways that you can retake your freedom and live the life of happiness that you deserve. Is escaping easy? No. Is it worth it? Absolutely. Your choice is none other than that of freedom or a slow, miserable, spiritual, and emotional death.

A strong word of caution must be emphasized before we begin to share how to escape a manipulative situation. Manipulative people are dangerous and devious. They will often stop at nothing to regain control of a situation. For such people, their victim escaping their clutches represents the ultimate loss of control. Many manipulators will stop at absolutely nothing to restore things to the way they want. If they find out that this is not possible, they may resort to acts of violence, stalking, and other forms of extremely dangerous criminal behavior.

That is not to say that these people cannot be escaped from—quite the opposite. Thousands of people each year find the courage and strength to take their life back. By following the advice of this, you will be able to experience the joy of your escape without running the risks that come with escaping in the wrong way.

Before the Escape

The exact nature of your escape from a manipulative person, and situation, depends heavily upon the type of manipulator you find yourself with and the details of the situation. However, every escape has in common is the need to plan very carefully before carrying it out. A well-planned escape makes all the difference between success and failure. Also, more importantly, planning makes the difference between danger and safety. So let's discover how to plan properly.

The first thing to realize when planning an escape is that very few people must know about it beforehand. People have a way of being unable to keep secrets or giving away the wrong information to the wrong person. Even if you tell people and they have your best intentions in mind, they may accidentally let the wrong thing slip at the wrong time.

There is also another key reason for telling as few people as possible about what you have planned. Many manipulators do not respect personal boundaries in any way whatsoever. They may go through your phone, your email, and your social media regularly without you having any idea. If they discover what you are planning, then you are placing yourself in a position of immense physical danger.

Even if you think that your manipulator is not going through your phone or your social media and that you have covered your tracks by deleting messages, there is no way that you can be sure. Did you know that software exists, which can be discretely installed on a PC or phone and allows someone to spy on you in real-time? As you are typing, each button you press could be being transmitted directly to your manipulator. There is no way you would know this is happening, and therefore there is no clear way to protect against it.

That is not to say that you should not tell anyone what you are planning. Rather, it is important to tell one trusted person only. This could be a best friend or a member of your family. You must trust this person with your life, as this is effectively what is at stake. You need to know this person will not let anything slip, even accidentally. The reason for telling them is that they can first support you through the process in any way you need, and secondly so that if anything goes wrong, they can inform the police what has happened and who is responsible.

Choosing the right person to let know what you are up to is only the first stage of the planning process. It is also absolutely vital to choose a physical place you can escape to and spend some time in the aftermath of your escape. This, ideally, will be somewhere out of town, preferably as far away as possible. This is because the manipulator is likely to look everywhere they can think of in the aftermath of you escaping the situation. The place you choose should be far away geographically and somewhere that the manipulator will not be able to figure out easily.

Preparing financially for life without a manipulator is another key aspect of planning. This can be very difficult as some types of manipulators are incredibly controlling when it comes to finances. Ideally, you will have one to two months' expenses saved up and be able to access them in a way that will not arouse suspicion. If this is not possible, your one trusted friend or family member should

be asked to help you out. You will be able to repay them after you have got clear of the situation. This is just a temporary measure. If you are in a situation where you live with your manipulator and want to move out, planning to take the things you need with you is important, but difficult. Anything that is replaceable should be left behind. Only essential things like valuable jewelry, identity documents, and other similar things should be taken. Ideally, you should only take as many things as you can fit into one bag. This makes the practical side of the escape much easier.

In the period leading up to your escape, you should put together a duffel bag or similar sized bag of new purchases from outside of the home. For example, you should pack some underwear, clothes, toiletries, and other similar items. They should not be taken from the home as their absence would likely arouse suspicion. Instead, they should all be new purchases. When you have carefully put together your bag, it is vital to find a safe place to store it. Some good ideas for such places include with your one trusted person or at some kind of rental locker space, such as a gym locker.

The above steps are the essentials you need to consider when planning your escape from a manipulative situation. There may be other steps you need to consider in light of your particular scenario, or some of the above ideas may not apply if you are sure to follow the advice, though. You are putting yourself in a position of preparedness and safety ahead of your escape.

Now that you have made practical preparations for your escape, it's time to plan the escape itself.

The preceding of this gave you all of the information you need to make some preparations ahead of your escape. While essential, it is not enough. Equally, if not more important, is to plan the actual escape. This includes the escape's nature, the escape's timing, and what you will do if something goes wrong. Having a clear plan in mind for the period after the escape is also essential. After the escape, this is often the most difficult time as the manipulator will know what has happened and look for revenge.

The first key step in this process is understanding exactly what an escape means to you. Every situation is different, and not all of them require a dramatic escape, which involves hiding out in some remote location. We will now look at some of the more appropriate escape methods depending on the type of manipulative situation you are trying to get away from. Suppose you are with one of the more serious types of relationship manipulators.

Suppose you are with one of the more serious types of relationship manipulators, such as someone who is violent, or gaslighting, or denying reality. In that case, it is vital to put physical distance between yourself and your manipulator. This is because these types of manipulators are the ones who will cross the line into violence and even murder if they are provoked. This is the most serious type of manipulative situation you can find yourself in, so make sure to leave nothing to chance when attempting to escape it. Some types of relationship manipulators are less dangerous, but you still should err on the side of caution. For example, suppose the person you are with manipulates you through lying and minimizing. In that case, you may not need to plan such a dramatic and comprehensive escape from this type of scenario. It may be enough to break up with such a person from a distance and make sure they know you will go to the police if they attempt to remain in contact with you.

Other types of situations require a different approach. If you are stuck in a manipulative workplace situation, you may find that changing jobs is the only way you can get out. It may be tempting to quit in the heat of the moment, but this is the wrong way to go about it. It is vital to have another job, known as a parachute job, lined up before you quit. Otherwise, you will face serious financial trouble after quitting the manipulative situation. Schedule interviews for days off from the office and consider using vacation time for all your new job interviews into two weeks. This can allow the job search process to be less stressful for you.

Conclusion

A healthy life with a narcissist is impossible. They do not know how to communicate with others in a way that is not manipulative. This is likely because as a child, they could not get their needs met by asking for them and had to go about it in an underhanded way, and as an adult, they continue this behavior. They will likely use these stories of childhood tragedies as a way of playing on your sympathy and getting you not to leave them. You can feel compassion for what they endured as a child, but you owe it to yourself not to tolerate abuse from who they have become as an adult.

It cannot be stressed enough how important it is that a survivor does not contact the narcissist. This means they cannot share phone calls, messages, or visit this person. It will only be detrimental to their mental health and put them right back into the position they worked so hard to get out of. They need to keep themselves out of the risk of breaking no contact.

This means their time needs to be filled with something else, so they won't have time to think about and contact the person they are trying to distance themselves from. This is the time to make new friends and reconnect with old ones. Taking up a new hobby or a class will take up your time and introduce you to new people.

Everyone who dealt with a covert narcissist knows the pain, toxicity, and hardships such an individual brings. As a result of being exposed to narcissistic abuse for a prolonged period, victims, future survivors face many challenges. They are faced with a great task: to leave it all behind and heal from what has transpired due to that relationship. Healing from abuse is never easy as it leaves deep marks on one's personality and diminishes their wellbeing. Covert narcissism is a set of destructive behavioral patterns that harm everyone involved with a person who harbors these behaviors. Unfortunately, because it is a personality disorder that is very much conceived, there are no proven ways to foresee you are dealing with one unless you've experienced being abused by a narcissist in your past.

Hard to diagnose, covert narcissists, because they are so well-liked and accepted in society represent a real threat to everyone they are involved with, as their destructive patterns, manipulation techniques, and controlling behavior can be extremely damaging to one's mental, physical, and emotional body. Being part of the Cluster B spectrum, covert narcissism represents a real danger to one's sense of self, self-worth, and mental health in general. It is threatening, disturbing, which is why a healing process for those who suffered from narcissistic abuse is a lengthy process that is never light and easy.

One of the most important things to do to heal from narcissistic abuse is to create and strengthen interpersonal relationships with others. You need to be focused on something outside of the relationship between you and a toxic person. If a bond does not replace the bond you break with them with someone else, it will be effortless to break no contact.

Realizing what led you to the place you are now is the first step to getting to a different one. Many times those who get into prolonged relationships with a narcissist, were raised by one. In reality, they were most likely raised by two. One parent was the overt narcissist who victimized the child with their rage, while the other parent allowed their child to be mistreated.

You have every right to be angry with a parent who mistreated you. However, you also need to permit yourself to be angry with the parent who kept that parent in the house and refused to leave them. This is a natural feeling, and you cannot feel guilty about it. Even if there were extenuating circumstances, the parent who allowed you to be exposed to narcissistic abuse throughout your upbringing did not do right by you. You probably also had to be a therapist for them. They needed to vent to you so that they could go on another day.

They will talk of the burden they bore for you, but there was also a burden you bore. Often, the child carries the heaviest weight throughout the entire family in a dysfunctional situation. There were probably times this parent turned the narcissistic parent's anger away from you and onto them, but there were also most likely times when they couldn't handle it anymore, and so it was "your turn" to deal with it. That act was abuse from them. A family is not supposed to be a dynamic to where there is a parent who flies into rages, and the child has to take the brunt of it on days when the other parent has had all they can stand.

A child who grew up with a parent who was prone to angry outbursts might internalize that behavior. Not realizing their parent's behavior came from within, they will think they were responsible for it. This theory will be confirmed by the fact that sometimes making themselves as small as possible, groveling, and going along with whatever the parent wanted would give them a reprieve. When this child grows into an adult, they will think they are responsible for other people's anger. They will feel a sense of guilt when another person gets angry and insults them. They will think, had they not done something wrong. They wouldn't be getting treated like this.

When a person has had long-term dealings with a narcissist, they come out of it with wounds that will take time and work to heal. There is an argument that a form of PTSD forms after suffering this type of abuse. Anxiety management is something you will need to learn while recovering from narcissistic abuse. Studies have shown that people are breaking away from a relationship with a narcissist exhibit symptom reminiscent of post-traumatic stress disorder.

They are hyper-vigilant because they never knew what would set off the narcissistic rage. People who are recovering from narcissistic abuse invariably have high levels of anxiety. They are traumatized by the way they have been treated. This is why it is essential to seek ongoing treatment for a little while after breaking free from psychological abuse.

While there is anxiety, there is also a feeling of numbness. This is another aspect of trauma. You cannot handle the sheer amount of stress you are under from the house's amount of tension. To feel all of it would be overwhelming to feel, so you choose not to feel it and then go into survival mode. Your mind is on getting through the situations that are thrown at you throughout the day.

There is a sad reality that people who were raised by a narcissist has to face. They have to watch out for narcissistic tics, also called fleas. These terms are used to refer to the tendencies they learned from their narcissistic caregiver. It is a way they further damage the children under their care. It is not enough to put them through the wringer that is narcissistic abuse. They also, whether it is conscious or not, try to teach their children narcissism. It can become a legacy if the child does not monitor their behavior as an adult. Humans respond to their environment and learn from the examples set for them by their caregivers.

Before you start to panic, be reassured, a tic does not mean you have become a narcissist. It means you have learned certain behaviors from those who raised you, as we all do. You are not a bad person because you were told lies as a child.

Think about it this way. A person raised by people who held prejudices against a specific religious or ethnic group would have been taught incorrect lessons about an entire population of people.

Their family went through a lot of trouble to program this person into thinking similarly to them. When you are a small child, you think your own family is a representation of all families. However, when you get out into the world, you will start to notice there are beliefs your family held that are not shared by other people. In the case of a person raised by a prejudiced family, they would have to learn some harsh truths about how they were raised.

They would discover that the belief they had always been taught to have was frowned upon by society and morally incorrect. It would be a complicated process for them to shed this thought process and take on a healthier one because our minds do not have switches that can be turned back and forth at our convenience. The person would go through a most likely lifelong journey of monitoring their biases and recognize when the old thought patterns were trying to creep their way back in.

Now let's apply this lesson to a person who had picked up a narcissistic tic from a parent. Melissa's mother was a covert narcissist. She had a very manipulative way of navigating through her relationships with others and yet would portray herself as a victim. As covert narcissists tend to do, she would seek out the company of overt narcissists. She would choose the same type of man to start a relationship with over and over again and be just as devastated every time these men let her down in the same ways as the ones did.

It is difficult to make connections in a situation when you are going through it personally. Melissa did not realize the similarities between her behaviors and that of her mother. When she thought about her, she felt a deep-seated resentment because she gave her a difficult childhood. When she started cognitive behavioral therapy, she began to realize her relationship patterns went the same way as her mother did—abrupt and ending chaotically. Her therapist reminds her that a child sees what is presented to them as normal.

They think the example their parents set for them is representative of how it is supposed to be and what everyone else does. She comes to realize she doesn't know what a healthy relationship looks like. She decides to take a break from dating until she learns how to choose better partners, be a better partner herself, and navigate through relationships in a more productive way. She realized she had developed thought patterns that were wrong due to her raising and is now working towards transforming these beliefs into healthier ones. That is the goal of cognitive-behavioral therapy.

www.ingramcontent.com/pod-product-compliance
Lightning Source LLC
Chambersburg PA
CBHW071120030426
42336CB00013BA/2154